Lights

Camera

Fashion

Modeling 101
Fundamental of Modeling

Chante Jones

Editor: Tosha Smith Mills

Photography/Cover: Alexander Le'Jo

ISBN: 9781076050878

Since I was six years old, I knew that I wanted to grace the runaway with my presence as a fashion model. As my mom would scroll through the channels looking for something interesting for me to watch, we would always run across pageants that JonBenet Ramsey was a participant of. As young as she was, she became my idol. Not knowing much about her, I would always say "Momma, I am going to be just like her."

I started modeling at a very young age; I mastered it and in this journal, I am going to share every tip that I possibly know. So what makes a successful model? It is not as glamourous as it seems. Being beautiful and photogenic is not what will help you be successful in this daunting industry.

I will share the pros and cons of my extensive observation of what can make you, but what can also break you in the modeling world. This is an inspirational journal for any and every person who would like to tap into the modeling industry.

Let this serve as a foundation – your own personal bible in the field of modeling. Remember that the lights are life, the camera is passion and everyone loves Fashion. You just have to master the journey. -Chante

This Journal Belongs To

_____

Name

_____

Contact Number

MODELING 101

"Modeling is a profession where your worth is tied up with looks." – Christy Turlington

When you think about a model or modeling, the first that comes to mind is a Runway Model. But there are so many types of modeling. Being a runway model limits who you are and what type of modeling that you do.

Modeling has been around since the beginning of time. Painters and sculptures would use models as their muses, and copy what they see into their sculptures.

Models come in all shapes and sizes and there is no particular model. Modeling is a job. All models are basically there to sell and brand a product.

THE TYPES OF MODELING:

High Fashion Modeling: High fashion modeling is also known as editorial modeling. High fashion modeling also known as supermodels can be found in Vogue, Glamour, Harper's Bazaar, and Elle. Models are also seen walking the runway for major fashion designers such as Gucci, Versace, Calvin Klein, Chanel and many others.

Runway Modeling: Runaway models are models that have really unique facial features and characteristics and poses to display clothing by walking along a narrow stage in front of an audience.

Glamour Modeling: Glamour modeling is modeling for photos with an exotic theme, bikini, and lingerie. You can see glamour models in Playboy, and is also becoming very popular on the internet. The glamour modeling industry has become very huge and can be found on the internet. While fashion modeling often requires a very specific thin body, glamour modeling prefers curves. While fashion modeling happens mostly in New York, Miami and Los Angeles, glamour modeling can happen anywhere.

Plus Size Modeling: There are many stores that only focus on plus size clothing, and only want plus size models. Plus size models are generally a size 10 and up and generally 5'8" to 5'10".

Body Part Modeling: Body part modeling belongs in both fashion and commercial modeling. This is a parts of the body that is used in photographs. Usually body part models will specialize in just one part of the body such as hands, feet, legs, ears, or neck. All of the parts being used must be wrinkle free, clean, clear skin and great nails.

Commercial Modeling: Commercial Modeling represents everything that is not fashion and is not glamour. The purpose is to sell a product, idea, or service.

Catalog Modeling: Models for catalogs can be anyone depending on what the basis of the what the catalog is for and what product or service is being sold.

Promotional Modeling: Promotional models are hired to hand out literature at trade shows and/or stores. Promotional models are usually very attractive people that people will stop and listen to about the sale of a product.

Fitness Modeling: Fitness models is specific to magazines that focus on health, fitness or nutrition. Models usually need to have toned and strong bodies.

Advertisement Modeling: Depending on the service or product being sold in the advertisement, different types of modeling will be used.

MODELING SCHOOLS:

Do you need to attend a modeling school?

A modeling school will like any other secondary school. A modeling school help you hone your skills to be better at what you would like to do. Modeling schools are different from modeling agencies. Agencies will develop your modeling skills if they feel you have what it takes to make them money. Modeling schools will teach you specific modeling skills such as your walk, creating portfolios, posing in front of the camera, applying makeup, and the business of modeling. Although these skills are good to have, they do not guarantee you a job in modeling.

Most of the instructors at the modeling schools are graduate of the schools that they are currently teaching and are not modeling professionally at all themselves.

Most real modeling agencies would prefer that you do not go to school. You will get the training you need on the job or by your agents for free.

Modeling schools can be very expensive; this is a business. They make money on services that they sell to you, and then get agencies to come to their school to scout out talent. When this happens, they congratulate the model and pass this information on to their potential students. It makes them look very good.

Most great models have not been to modeling school. 99.9% of models get their careers started in other ways, like submitting a portfolio to qualified agents and scouts. This does not mean that modeling school has no value, like anything else, you must be weary. However, for good training on becoming a model, seek out a professional model in the business who can serve as a mentor.

MODELING SEARCHES/CONVENTIONS

Model searches/conventions will advertise on the radio, on television, in the newspapers or on the internet. You will hear an ad on the radio that sounds something like that "a casting director for Disney will be at the Marriott Hotel searching for actors and models to be on the next show." People who respond to these ads are told about an upcoming search event, and some of the attendees are invited to go. The companies make an effort to screen out people who obviously have no hope of being selected by a model or talent agency, but not all are very scrupulous, and a wide net is cast. Sometimes anyone who is willing to pay to attend is allowed to, no matter what they are like.

At most events, the "talent" will outnumber the "model" applicants. The total number of attendees needs to be several hundred just for the company to make their expenses, so typically a model search will have over a thousand model and talent contestants.

In total there may be 30-50 or more model and talent agents doing the scouting at these events. Most will be from major market cities: New York, Los Angeles, Miami and perhaps Chicago. There may also be a small number of local agencies in attendance.

Usually a search is a two or three day affair. The first day may be taken up by various types of training and seminars (all offered at additional cost) conducted by industry professionals. They will usually have a photo booth set up too, so attendees can purchase headshots at the event. The second day may involve more seminars and some "competitions". Each competitor will be given a number on a large badge, which they wear so agents will know who they are.

For "talent" the competitions may be as simple as giving each of the hundred or so contestants a short (15-30 second) opportunity to perform a monologue, a runway walk or talent of their choice for the talent agents. Then everyone All the agents (model and talent agencies both) assemble around a runway, and the talent will walk down it at 15 second intervals or so for a chance to be seen.

At both the runway and talent competitions agents have "callback sheets" that they use to write down the number of people they are interested in seeing later. At the end of each competition these are turned in to the search firm staff.

Following the competitions, and after a break for the staff to compile callback requests, "callbacks" will be announced for agents to meet with the requested talent. The agents will be at tables in one or more large halls, and those requested talent with callbacks let into the halls. They may have to stand in line for a while, depending on the number of people an agency has called back, but they will get an opportunity for a brief personal interview at the callback.

In many ways conventions are similar to the searches, but they differ in important respects. Searches are "retail" events – they market directly to individuals who want to be models, actors and singers. Conventions are "wholesale" events. Almost all of their contestants are brought by modeling schools from around the country (or even internationally). The school receives a part of the model's fee for attending, and for many schools, taking people to the model conventions is a large part of their income.

The largest of the conventions typically gets 2,000-2,500 contestants; smaller ones may be in the range of 800-1,000. Where a search event may attract 30-50 agencies, a large convention may have 200 or more different agencies scouting at the event, and they will have a substantial number of international agencies represented. There is roughly an even split between model and talent agencies. The great majority of the model agencies scouting at a convention will be editorial fashion agencies from major market cities.

The convention itself is usually longer and more involved than at a search event, although the same basic things happen. There will be seminars, contests, group events where schools compete against each other, photographers taking pictures to sell, and runway or other opportunities for models and talent to briefly come to the attention of the agents. And there will be callbacks as well, handled in much the same way as at search events.

The modeling schools, conventions and searches all deliver what they promise. You will be seen by modeling agencies, and could be selected by them.

If you have the look of a model, take a great portfolio with a photographer who specializes in modeling and send a selective amount of pictures to various agencies.

A precaution, if you attend one of these modeling conventions or searches, if you are picked, are you prepared to move to the city in which the modeling agency is? If not, do no waste your time.

WHAT MAKES YOU A GREAT MODEL?

_____

_____

_____

_____

_____

_____

_____

_____

_____

_____

_____

_____

_____

_____

_____

_____

_____

_____

_____

_____

_____

_____

_____

_____

_____

_____

_____

HOW ARE YOU DIFFERENT?

PREPARING TO BE A MODEL-WHAT ARE YOU DOING?

PRACTICE MAKES PERFECT

"An aspiring model should never stop learning or working for what they want." – Chante Jones

When you are a beginner to the modeling industry, practice will only make you better. Models need to look as comfortable, natural, and confident as they possibly can. You must practice your walk, facial expressions, facial angles, poses and smile so that when the spotlight lands on you, you know exactly what to do. You must also learn fluent movement, and breathing in and out can make a huge difference in assisting with facial expressions in finding the light with your eyes and smize (smile with your eyes). Look at the modeling television shows, go to fashion shows, search the internet, listen to other models speak, adhere to their verbiage and posture, learn how to walk like them and study the craft every day.

WARMING UP

After practicing, you should know what angles work for you. Warming up means to get ready to shine. Play your favorite song, develop a routine for each song, move around, dance, stretch, and do workouts to keep your blood flowing. Remember to find the light in your eyes, open them, then smize. All of these things sets the tone and develops energy. This can make or break you. Stretch those muscles and move gracefully like a ballerina.

I remember going to a casting; I was very confident with my wild curly hair, sparkly one piece bathing suit and black wedge heels. I walked into a room full of people and ignored every scare. I was really nervous. When they called my name to walk, I totally bombed it. I was not prepared at all; I was so nervous and in my head I was constantly telling myself "Chante, you are walking crooked." Who knew how hard it was to walk straight, I have been doing it all my life. Everyone in the room was looking at me and no one said a word. Casting made me walk again to Beyonce's song "Who run the world" and of course I ripped the runway, but if I would have practiced more, I would have killed it without music. I could not wait to get home to practice on a straight line with tape; I made sure to take my time. It is so important to practice every day so you do not get in the casting room and humiliate yourself.

MIRROR WORK

I have a big nose, and naturally, I have trained myself to be cautious of that area. I also keep my head up so my crown does not slip. Practicing for the camera should be easy and fun, it is all about getting in the mirror and working the frame. Check your strong poses, and sharp angles in the face; choose your best profile and stick to it. Learn to utilize your flaws that God has given you and be confident in using them.

Do not just focus on your face, get in front of a full length mirror and practice your walk and poses. Practice posing in the mirror and quickly rule out anything that looks awkward and unnatural and instead, focus on your flattering and natural poses that photographers, model scouts and agents are sure to love.

Models benefit from practicing their poses and looking in the mirror and practicing their smile and expression. The work you put it in practicing your poses and expressions will save industry professionals a lot of time in critiquing you. These industry professionals sometimes see hundreds of people a day which means they know talent when they see it. They know who have practiced it, focused on it, and mastered it. This will also demonstrate how serious you are in getting this job.

Just a few minutes of preparing each day will expand your work ethic and have a positive effect on the success of your modeling career.

<u>HOW ARE YOU GETTING PREPARED?</u>

PRAYER WILL HELP YOU GET READY FOR PERFECT!

_____

_____

_____

_____

_____

_____

_____

_____

_____

_____

_____

_____

_____

_____

_____

_____

_____

_____

_____

_____

_____

_____

_____

_____

THE RIGHT TEAM

"I don't trust words, I trust pictures." - Gilles Perres

CHOOSING A PHOTOGRAPHER

Photographers are important, in fact they are just as important as the model. The photographer and model both deserve to be paid for their work; in exchange for pictures, some photographers will photograph for free. In almost any case, if a photographer ask you to take pictures, it will be in exchange for photos. If you are asked by a reputable agency to take pictures, it is important to seek out a photographer who specializes in taking modeling and fashion portfolios. Every photographer is not experienced in fashion and modeling photography; please seek out one who is. Agencies can tell the difference.

Interview photographers and ask to see his/her work. Look at the quality of his work and if he does not have social media or a website displaying his work, please seek out one who does. Google him/her to check out their style of images. Because photography is so competitive and fierce, it will not be hard to find one, but may be hard to chose one.

MODEL USAGE LICENSES

You do not own any of the pictures unless you pay for them. The photographer owns the copyright, and the right to publish the pictures. All that can be changed if the photographers gives you a release in a written contract. To publish them yourself, you will need usage license from the photographer.

I am not trying to scare you, but I am trying to inform you that if a photographer gives you a picture, make sure you have permission to make copies of it, put it on your website or use it for any reason.

If you want to retouch your pictures, you would have to get permission from him as well, however, you should never work with a photographer who you have paid that will not retouch or edit picture.

COMP CARDS/PORTFOLIOS

A part of being prepared is to know that it is very imperative to have a portfolio and comp cards on you at all times. Your comp card is your business card and is also your selling tool. Quality is essential over quantity. You must have quality images. You would rather have four great images instead of fourteen basic images. When choosing photos, try to chose photos with different angles and different expressions. You do not want four of the same photo with the same facial expressions. You want to give the agency that you are interviewing with a variety of great photographs to look at. Once chosen, some of the larger agencies will send you to a reputable photographer to have a photoshoot done at their expense.

THE RIGHT AGENCY

Once you have studied and prepared to be a model, you have taken the right portfolio, and confident that you are ready to model professionally, of course, choosing a modeling agency, immediately comes to mind.

Seeking a modeling agency is not hard, but choosing the right agency is. First of all, you have to chose an agency that has a well written contract that will explain the terms and provisions to you. You want an agency that will advise you, treat you fairly, believe in you, and will be just right for YOU! First of all, you must first do your research and ask yourself if you are willing to do what it take to become the model that you have always dreamed of, even if it means moving to another state or even another country.

When interviewing agencies, here are some questions you may want to ask:

1. Where are you geographically located?
2. Will I have to move to where you are?
3. Will you pay for my test shoots?
4. I know that you cannot guarantee me work, but how often will I go on go-sees?
5. Is your agency considered a boutique agency or larger agency?
6. Who are some of your clients?
7. What type of jobs do you book for your models?
8. What are your commission rates?
9. Are your contracts exclusive?
10. How many years have your agency been in business?

Here are some red flags when interviewing an agency. If any of these red flags come out, run immediately and seek out another agency.

1. Asking for money before they find you work.
2. Guarantee of work.
3. Being required to use a certain photographer that you must pay for.
4. Insisting on modeling classes.
5. Application or audition fees.

"ANYTHING THAT HINDERS YOU FROM MOVING FORWARD, DETACH YOURSELF."

PREPARING FOR

GO-SEES

"Preparing is a way to say who you are without having to speak" - Chante Jones

Every model gets excited when she receives that first call for a "go-see." A "go-see" is to modeling as an audition is to an actor. The go-see is the appointment for a model to be seen and interviewed for a modeling job. It allows the casting director or company representatives to see and meet the model to determine if the model is right for the job. When your agency calls, they are calling because you fit the specifics of what the company is looking for. To be successful in this industry, you must ask all the right questions to make sure that you are right for the job. Even though you may fit the specs, it may not be something that you want to do. Your agency will give you the following:

1. The client and product;
2. The dates of the shoot;
3. The location of the shoot;
4. How much the job pays;
5. The wardrobe; and
6. What you will portray and the usage.

Once you decide to take the audition for the job, it is now for you to get prepared. You then ask the following questions:

1. Where is the go-see?
2. When is it?
3. Who shall I see?

Please keep in mind that you have been given privileged information, so it is imperative that you keep this confidential. Unless you are minor, you should always attend alone. If your agency did not discuss what you should wear, please wear the basics which is a basic tank top or shirt, jeans, and heels. Your clothing should be form fitting, not extremely tight and should be neutral colors. Please do not over accessorize, and wear light makeup if any at all. The representatives/casting directors need to see who you are and therefore, you should be as natural as possible.

Your Model Bag

Always bring your model bag with you. A model bag is both essential and crucial. Essential because it is a necessary and crucial because without it, you are lost. Make sure your modeling bag have the following:

1. Nude/black undies;
2. Nude/black heels;
3. Soap;
4. Towel;
5. Deodorant;
6. Wipes;
7. Makeup;
8. Change of clothes; and
9. Snacks.

What Happens at the Go-See?

At the go-see, you present yourself to the casting director and/or the company representative to see if you are the right match for their product or service. Make sure that you arrive on time, have a comp-card, headshot and/or portfolio or whatever your agency has asked you to present. Once you arrive, sign in, sit there quite and stay off of your cell phone. If you must take a call, please excuse yourself from the casting office and get back there as quickly as possible.

So you booked the job!

Once your agent calls you to give you the great news of booking the job, you are about to get to do what models all want to do.

1. **Be prepared.** For men this means having a haircut, ideally out a week before the shoot. For women it means have your hair attractively styled in a manner consistent with the shoot. For everyone it means knowing before you get there what role you will play. Unlike fashion shoots, most commercial shoots require you to have a wardrobe appropriate to the shoot (a small selection of clothing and shoes that fits the role you will play). It should be clean, pressed and ready. Even if you have been told that there will be a makeup artist present, bring your own makeup. Get a good night's sleep!

2. Show up on time! This is the single most important rule of all. If you are late, you are liable for all the overtime you just contributed to – and at the huge hourly rates of other models, the photographer, stylist and others, you *really* don't want to have to pay that. And "on time" doesn't mean the time scheduled it means 10-15 minutes earlier, so you have a chance to get your makeup on and ready yourself for the shoot. At the appointed time you need to be able to step out on the set, ready to shoot. If a makeup artist is provided for complex makeup you can do this "on the clock"

but sometimes a scheduled makeup artist is cancelled, and you need to be ready if that happens.

3.   Introduce yourself to everyone. Or at least everyone who seems to want to meet you, and that you won't interfere with. These are the people who can make you look bad or good, who may or may not want to hire you for the follow-on TV commercial that goes with your print ad for instance. Do what you can to help them look good in a pleasant way, and they will return the favor.

4.   Do not discuss rates or terms. If someone on the set brings these things up, politely refer the question to your agency. Never change the terms of a shoot without your agent being involved.

5.   Shoot what was booked. But no more than what was booked. If you are doing a TV commercial and someone asks to "just take a couple of still shots," call your agency immediately. Never put yourself in the position of having to be the one to say no, but do not allow any shooting beyond what was booked without your agent's approval. If you do, you may give up rights to thousands of dollars worth of usage fees, especially if the photographer asks you to sign his release.

6. Sign the voucher. When the shoot is over you should fill out the portion of the voucher that shows how much time you worked, and the rights being purchased at the time of the shoot. Time is computed from the time the shoot is scheduled to start, until the last shot is taken. Lunch and other breaks are included in the time. Sign the voucher, have the photographer or client's representative sign it, and take one copy for yourself and one for the agency.

PRAYER IS THE KEY. PRAY BEFORE YOU ATTEND ANY GO-SEES!

KID MODELING

"Children are our future we must take care of them with maximum effort." -Naomi Campbell

In many ways child modeling is similar to adult modeling, but there are some special considerations that apply only to children. There is a market for kids, but it is in the larger markets like Miami, Los Angeles, New York and Milan. Children and babies work is very rare, unless you live in that market already, I would not waste time or money relocating to that market. Here are a few tips for parents to follow in pursuing modeling for their child or children:

1. The child should be small for their age. That lets them plat younger roles in advertising, and have more life experience and maturity than a child of the age they are playing.
2. The need to be comfortable around adults, and have outgoing personalities.
3. They need to be well behaved and take direction very well.
4. Should be taking acting, singing and dance classes. DO NOT ENROLL THEM IN MODELING CLASSES.
5. The child has to want it. If the parents want it more than the child, it is a bad idea and withdraw immediately.
6. Parents need to be supportive and not critical and/or pushy.

7. This is a job. A parent must be available to take their child to all go-sees.
8. Good grades are essential as the kid may need to be off of school from time to time.
9. Children do not need a portfolio, but does not professional quality pictures.
10. Kids change on any given day. Keep the agency updated on tooth loses or braces. It is not a good idea if a child shows up for a job and has changed drastically from how their pictures are presented.

Always remember that while their beautiful faces get them through the door, their personality is what will give them staying power.

GOALS FOR YOUR CHILDREN IN THE MODELING INDUSTRY

_____

_____

_____

_____

_____

_____

_____

_____

_____

_____

_____

_____

_____

_____

_____

_____

_____

_____

_____

_____

_____

_____

_____

TIPS FOR MODELS

"Take care of yourself, be healthy, and always believe you can be successful in anything you truly want."

-Alessandra Ambrosio

"Taking care of your skin is essential for any model. After using natural products, I will never use chemicals again. Lemon, honey and baking soda is for active acne lemons and baking soda will burst and pimple. Honey and fresh lemon peels dark marks of hyperpigmentation. The acid in the lemon peels away the marks and honey adds moisture back into your skin. To exfoliate, I use wet sugar with water and I gently scrub my face. Be sure to wear sunscreen."

_____

_____

_____

_____

_____

_____

_____

_____

_____

_____

_____

_____

_____

_____

_____

_____

_____

_____

_____

"Models must adapt to every environment without complaints, because just how you are feeling, so does everyone else, but who is complaining?"

_____

_____

_____

_____

_____

_____

_____

_____

_____

_____

_____

_____

_____

_____

_____

_____

_____

_____

_____

_____

_____

_____

"It should be your duty to have some sort of impact on someone's life."

"A lousy photographer can make or break you."

_____

_____

_____

_____

_____

_____

_____

_____

_____

_____

_____

_____

_____

_____

_____

_____

_____

_____

_____

_____

_____

"Time waits on no one; use your time wisely."

_____

_____

_____

_____

_____

_____

_____

_____

_____

_____

_____

_____

_____

_____

_____

_____

_____

_____

_____

_____

_____

_____

"Peace is so easy to find. The question is do you want it."

_____

_____

_____

_____

_____

_____

_____

_____

_____

_____

_____

_____

_____

_____

_____

_____

_____

_____

_____

_____

_____

_____

_____

"Everyone does not deserve your time or energy."

"Continue to educate yourself."

"Patience is learned through trying times."

_____
_____
_____
_____
_____
_____
_____
_____
_____
_____
_____
_____
_____
_____
_____
_____
_____
_____
_____
_____
_____
_____
_____
_____
_____

"Start each shoot or show with a prayer."

_____

_____

_____

_____

_____

_____

_____

_____

_____

_____

_____

_____

_____

_____

_____

_____

_____

_____

_____

_____

_____

"There are more no's than yes's. Hang in there."

_____

_____

_____

_____

_____

_____

_____

_____

_____

_____

_____

_____

_____

_____

_____

_____

_____

_____

_____

_____

_____

_____

_____

_____

"Modeling is a business, and as a model, you are your own business."

_____

_____

_____

_____

_____

_____

_____

_____

_____

_____

_____

_____

_____

_____

_____

_____

_____

_____

_____

_____

_____

_____

_____

"Confidence is the key."

_____

_____

_____

_____

_____

_____

_____

_____

_____

_____

_____

_____

_____

_____

_____

_____

_____

_____

_____

_____

_____

_____

_____

_____

"Look after your hair and skin."

"Keep your makeup at a minimum."

_____

_____

_____

_____

_____

_____

_____

_____

_____

_____

_____

_____

_____

_____

_____

_____

_____

_____

_____

_____

_____

_____

_____

_____

"Drink lots of water, hold on to a healthy diet, work out regularly, get sufficient sleep, and avoid cigarettes and alcohol."

_____
_____
_____
_____
_____
_____
_____
_____
_____
_____
_____
_____
_____
_____
_____
_____
_____
_____
_____
_____
_____
_____
_____
_____

"Stay prepared. Opportunities come and go."

"Always keep a pair of heels with you in case you get a spur of the moment go-see."

"Keep your nails clean and clear."

_____

_____

_____

_____

_____

_____

_____

_____

_____

_____

_____

_____

_____

_____

_____

_____

_____

_____

_____

_____

_____

_____

_____

_____

_____

_____

"Practice your facial expressions and walk for an hour a day."

_____

_____

_____

_____

_____

_____

_____

_____

_____

_____

_____

_____

_____

_____

_____

_____

_____

_____

_____

_____

_____

"Being stable is the best feeling in the world; the foundation of your life is important."

_____
_____
_____
_____
_____
_____
_____
_____
_____
_____
_____
_____
_____
_____
_____
_____
_____
_____
_____
_____
_____
_____

"Always know your size and measurements and be
honest about it."

_____

_____

_____

_____

_____

_____

_____

_____

_____

_____

_____

_____

_____

_____

_____

_____

_____

_____

_____

_____

_____

_____

_____

_____

_____

_____

_____

"Being true to yourself is your compass to a great life."

"Always keep your photos fresh."

_____

_____

_____

_____

_____

_____

_____

_____

_____

_____

_____

_____

_____

_____

_____

_____

_____

_____

_____

_____

_____

_____

_____

_____

_____

"Whether happy, serious or neutral, expressions are crucial."

Remember to smize."

_____

_____

_____

_____

_____

_____

_____

_____

_____

_____

_____

_____

_____

_____

_____

_____

_____

_____

_____

_____

_____

_____

_____

_____

_____

_____

"Study…Research….Learn….."

"Always show versatility."

"Never wear wedges on a go-see."

_____
_____
_____
_____
_____
_____
_____
_____
_____
_____
_____
_____
_____
_____
_____
_____
_____
_____
_____
_____
_____
_____
_____
_____
_____
_____
_____

"Keep your model bag equipped with any and everything that you will need for the day."

_____

_____

_____

_____

_____

_____

_____

_____

_____

_____

_____

_____

_____

_____

_____

_____

_____

_____

_____

_____

_____

_____

_____

_____

KEY TERMS

Booker - a booker is someone who works in a model agency and keeps track of which clients hire which models.

Bookout - Notification to your agent that you're not available for a casting or job, for either professional or personal reasons. You are not available at this time, the clients cannot book you during that time, you've "booked out."

Buyouts - This is the payment for the use of model pictures. Often this is negotiated on top of the dayrate and sometimes it's included. The type of use must be set (poster, advertisements, internet, TV etc.), as well as the run-time and the countries.

Calltime - The time at which a model must be at the location and ready to work.
Call Back / Recall - after the first casting a callback or recall is held to narrow down the selection process. It is not unusual to get a callback before getting a job or being turned down.

Casting - Castings are notices of modelling jobs which are made to models, casting agencies, or on modelling websites. They show details of the types of models required for an upcoming production. This could mean a call where every model can apply or a date on which (preselected) models introduce themselves to the client, who will then make the final decision. The client sets the requirements and makes his/her choice.

Casting Agency - Casting agencies are agencies specialized in finding talented people for different fields like modeling, singing, acting, dancing and others. They work similarly to scouts. They search for perspective persons that could participate in different kinds of projects like TV, photo, video, advertisement casting and others. Usually the models in a casting agency doesn't have an exclusive contract and can work for different agencies.

Casting Detail Sheet - Information sheet for the model, which contains all important information about a casting: calltime, direction, client etc.

Catwalk/Runway - Catwalk or runway describes a narrow, usually elevated platform that runs into an auditorium, used by models to demonstrate clothing and accessories during a fashion show.

Close Up - In film, television or photography a close-up tightly frames a person or an object. Close-ups are one of the standard shots used regularly along with medium shots and long shots.

Composite Card - Also referred to as a comp card, sedcard, (zedcard) or model business card. A composite card is a piece of card which is printed with at least two photos of you in various poses, settings, outfits and looks (the widest variety possible). It includes your name, your contact information, usually your agency's info and all your stats. Comp cards come in lots of different formats depending on the city, agency and the type of model you are. Agencies will usually issue comp cards for you after they sign you. A composite card serves as the latest and best of a model's portfolio and are used as a business card.

Contest - A contest in this case mostly refers to a model contest. This is an event in which models engage in competition against each other, often for a prize or similar incentive. Modelmanagement.com runs it's own international Fresh Faces contest annually.

Copyright - Copyright is the set of exclusive rights granted to the author or creator of an original work, including the right to copy, distribute and adapt the work. These rights can be licensed, transferred and/or assigned.

Cover Shooting - A photo shooting for a cover of a magazine. Depending on the magazine it has great significance for the awareness of the model.

Cuttings - Documented releases of a model in magazines, catalogs or other medias

Editorial - Photographs made to illustrate a story or idea within the context of a magazine. These are usually assigned by the magazine.

Fitting - The session that takes place before the photo shoot where the clothes to be modelled are fit onto the model. Based on the model's particulars, the clothes are usually altered to fit. When you go to a fitting, be prepared to stand around partially clothed all day long, in front of several people. These people will usually be stylists, seamstresses and designers. The fitting is often included in the day rate.

Go-See - A model's appointment to see a potential client, to present his book and his - or herself in person and to leave a good impression. Often a client keeps the models in mind for his next shoot/job.

Head Sheet - A poster displaying head shots and information about models represented by a modeling agency.

Lingerie - Lingerie is the word use for alluring undergarments.

Location - Any place where a shoot (photography or film) takes place. When you are on location, it means you are outside the controlled environment of the studio or soundstage and should prepare accordingly.

Make-Up Artist - A makeup artist (MUA) is an artist whose medium is the human body, applying makeup and prosthetics for theatrical, television, film, fashion, magazines and other similar productions including all aspects of the modeling industry.

Model Agency - A model agency is a company that represents fashion models, to work for the fashion industry. These agencies earn their income via commission, usually from the deal they make with the model or the client. The model agency presents the models to the clients, promotes them to foreign agencies and is in charge of the models chart, book, portfolio, buyouts, travel etc.

Model Release - A legal document provided by the client/photographer and signed by the model or agent. It gives permission to the photographer to use photographs taken at a particular sitting. If photographs are used without a release, or in a way different from what is stated in the release, then the model can sue for breach of contract.

New Faces - New Faces or newcomers are models who are new into business. They are just starting their career and usually don't have a professional book done.

Plus Size - Plus-size model is a term applied to a person who is engaged primarily in modeling plus-size clothing.

Plus-size models also engaged in work that is not strictly related to selling large-sized clothing, e.g., stock photography and advertising photography for cosmetics, household and pharmaceutical products and sunglasses, footwear and watches. Therefore plus-size models do not exclusively wear garments marketed as plus-size clothing. This is especially true when participating in fashion editorials for mainstream fashion magazines.

Polaroid - Polaroid photos is a special type of photos that are used in modeling business. Polaroids are usually needed for agencies or scouts to see the natural look of the model. This is something every model needs in their portfolio if they intend to be serious in this business. Modelmanagement.com offers professional polaroids for new models who require them or for professionals who need up to date polaroids.

Prints - Prints are printed negatives, the real photos.

Senior model - A senior model is a professional model in his 40s/50s/60s. As the average age is constantly raising, the advertisements go back more and more to older models to approach their target group. A senior models often has a good book as they can show a lot of experience or after easily being booked for ads they get publications from the beginning on.

Set - This is where the action of shoot takes place usually within a professional studio or within a location. It includes all the elements which make the shoot; for example the lighting, camera, art direction and art directed scenery.

Shooting - Shooting in general means the implementation of photo or film shoots.

Smize – Smiling with your eyes.

Stock Photos - Stock photography is the supply of photographs licensed for specific uses. It is used to fulfill the needs of creative assignments instead of hiring a photographer. Today, stock images are usually presented in searchable online databases, where they are then purchased and delivered online. Often, they are produced in studios using a wide variety of models posing as professionals, stereotypes, expressing stereotypical emotions and gesticulations or involving pets.

Stylist - The stylist is in charge of the outfit of the model and discussing at length with the photographer or director, about theme of the shoot.

Tearsheet - sometimes written 'Tear sheet' is a term used by Advertising agencies to denote a page cut or torn from a publication to prove to the client that the advertisement was published. Media buying agencies are often required by clients to provide tear sheets along with a post analysis of any advertising campaign.

Test Shooting/TFP - An agreement between the model and photographer to whereby they work for each other on a mutually beneficial basis. No fees other than sharing film-and-developing expenses are involved. They work together on a new idea or on their portfolios. The photographer provides a selection of prints from the shoot in recognition of the model's time commitment.

Usage - Models get paid for each different medium in which their photograph is used. These different mediums, or usages, may include: consumer magazines, trade magazines, product packaging, print ads, bus ads, subway ads, billboards, magazine covers, direct mail, magazine editorials, posters, catalogues, brochures, point-of-purchase (point-of-sale or p-o-p), annual reports, book covers, kiosk, (those big portable billboards that are towed around behind trucks), newspapers, etc. The model receives an additional fee for each usage the client buys. Usages also vary according to time and region. The longer the ad runs and the more markets in which it appears, all drive up the model's fee. The largest usage is the unlimited time usage, worldwide buyout. That means the client can plaster the photograph across every city in the world in every possible usage until the end of time.

Made in the USA
Columbia, SC
10 January 2020